GLIMPSES
OF
GOD

Kris Coleman and Larry Kennard

GLIMPSES OF GOD

Scripture taken from The Holy Bible, King James Version. Cambridge Edition: 1769; King James Bible Online, 2016. www.kingjamesbibleonline.org.

iUniverse books may be ordered through booksellers or by contacting:

iUniverse
1663 Liberty Drive
Bloomington, IN 47403
www.iuniverse.com
1-800-Authors (1-800-288-4677)

ISBN: 978-1-5320-2524-2 (sc)
ISBN: 978-1-5320-2525-9 (e)

Library of Congress Control Number: 2017909054

Print information available on the last page.

iUniverse rev. date: 06/27/2017

DEDICATION

First we would like to dedicate this book to God the Father of our Lord Jesus Christ, to Him belongs all the glory. To all of our family and friends who prayed for the completion of this book. The power of the Holy Spirit who fought for us and protected the contents of this book. May each person reading this book obtain the revelation of the power of God and the reality of a God who is real and loves us very deeply. May the advancement of the kingdom of God in your hearts and life increase daily along with your desire to know Him better.

CONTENTS

Preface...ix

Hidden Things Come to Light............................. 1

What is Seen of God 7

God in Creation...9

What is Seen of God Through Our Lord Jesus Christ 11

What is Seen by God..Our Faith 13

What is Seen by God Through His People 15

God's Plan for Man 17

... Blinded..19

Renewal of Sight 23

The Word of Our Testimonies............................27

Healing and Miracles..35

I am a Diamond..39

PREFACE

The following are questions that some may ask themselves concerning their established beliefs. Our challenge is to unravel some of the mysteries in response to the question we have been asked. Questions pertaining to "Who am I", "What am I here for" and "Does my life really matter". Some ask if I saw God would I believe in Him? The skeptics of the world say, I won't believe unless I see something to prove God is real. After all what is faith and why do I need it? All of us are unique and seldom reach the same conclusions on the matter of faith and God the same way.

This book will help you see and perceive Glimpses of God in your everyday existence. Our hope is to erase all doubt or uncertainty of His existence. What was hidden or not understood about God our creator and yourself will be revealed and no longer a mystery. We trust that this book will stir within each reader a desire to begin, renew or enrich your relationship with Him. You will begin to understand with more clarity why you were created, what you were designed for, who God is and why He is interested in you. He desires to personally reveal Himself unto you by exhibiting His majesty and glory; both of which you can be a partaker of right now today! You will also see and perceive with more clarity after reading Glimpses of God that you do matter to Him. The love He has for you is beyond anything you have ever imagined. God's intention from the very beginning was for mankind to have and enjoy a relationship with Him everyday.

Your journey of discovery will help you understand the purpose of your existence. Glimpses of God will help give you a reason to hope in your future knowing you are never alone, but in the constant care of a loving Creator.

are this smoke. God was in the smoke. Although we couldn't see the face of God, we saw the outline of His body which is the same shape as ours today. In the bible there was a servant and prophet of God called Moses who had a very intimate relationship with Him. It describes in Exodus chapter 33:17-23, how God told Moses that he would not be allowed to see the face of God because no mortal man can see His face and live. Instead God hid Moses in the cleft of a rock and allowed him to see the hind parts of His glory as He passed by. These biblical accounts are given to reveal glimpses of God and to help us understand that He is interested in us all and all that we do. God wants to illuminate our minds to perceive Him and His glory on earth. Larry and I could not see the face of God in the vision of the throne room. The smoke of His glory is mixed with the prayers of the saints while it was ascending up surrounding the altar of God. This will help you to understand how important our prayers and giving of thanks are to God. Nothing goes unnoticed

Once during our prayer time as Larry and I stood in the chapel, we saw these objects, which will refer to for now as orbs, that appeared behind each of us. The orbs looked like bright fiery opals, shimmering bright white, light blue and pinkish red in color. As we were praying our bodies, head first, began to be sucked into these orbs backwards like a vacuum. We became afraid not knowing what they were, where they came from or where they would take us. Our reaction once again was to say, "I'm not going in there". It was then I felt I had to use all of the strength of my spirit to force the orb to release my body from it's suction grip. Have you ever experienced trying to wake up or rise up out of your bed during sleep and felt some resistance? That is what this felt like. I actually had to wrestle to free myself from the pull of the orb. What seemed like a long time was a brief moment because we were in the spirit. Of course, Larry and I both were a bit shaken up by this unimaginable event.

That morning after arriving home, I was still pondering the events of that night wondering what those orbs Larry and I saw was all about. I got home and turned on the television to a channel I never watch. To my amazement there was a preacher on TV talking about what Larry and I just experienced that night. He called these orb shaped objects the portals of heaven. Now a portal is something used to transport you from one place or dimension to another. This preacher described the orbs exactly as we experienced them. He said they come to take people to heaven. My mouth fell open and I immediately called Larry because I was so excited. We began to praise God for making His glory known to us and thanked Him for allowing us to behold glimpses of His power. The possibility of a phenomenon of this magnitude to exist as the portals of heaven was awesome. Needless to say I was mad at myself for being fearful and allowing my fear to stop me from entering into the portal when I could have received greater glimpses of God.

God desires to give us greater and clearer revelations of Himself. The Lord has prepared good and great things for us. These glimpses of God should make Him more real to us. These glimpses can increase our appetite to know Him in a more personal and intimate way. Allow God to reveal more of Himself to you in your daily life. As you experience amazing visitations from the Lord, a desire to know Him better will increase. Remember God desires a relationship with you. Giving us glimpses of His marvelous and wondrous works will not only stir the Spirit from within but will also offer encouragement on this journey of receiving clearer revelation of Him in your daily life.

Unfortunately, these bodies of clay cannot contain all the power and glory of God presently. He covered His glory in the flesh of His Son, Jesus Christ, when He was on the earth. He then touched us flesh to flesh. Now, however, He must reveal Himself in part giving us glimpses.

WHAT IS SEEN OF GOD

We know in part, we see in part and prophesy in part.
1 Corinthians 13:9

What does it mean to get a glimpse of something? According to Webster's Dictionary, it means to get a partial or brief incomplete view. To peer or glance at something.

Here we will begin to reveal or unfold the different ways God gives us glimpses of Himself in everyday life. What unfolds is from our first beginnings to the wonderful ending God had planned for us from the beginning of time. It is sin, which is disobedience to God that has brought darkness to our minds. Sin also blinds, diminishes and clouds our vision, eclipsing the reality to the presence of God in our lives.

GOD IN CREATION

God from the beginning desired for us to see. This is why He said, "Let there be light". (Genesis 1:3). There must be light before we can see anything. This enables man to logically conclude that the earth must have been dark and void of light if it had to be created. I want you to see glimpses of God another way by beginning with looking at how our bodies are constructed and made. Take a moment and examine your hands, feet and eyes. No two people God ever created have the same fingerprints. You cannot help but admit what a marvelous creation you are. A creation well put together; arranged in a particular order. You are made after Gods image, after his likeness. Genesis 1:26 and 2 Corinthians 4:7). This revelation is one example of the love and power of The Almighty that we can see in earthen vessels. Here we are given insight or glimpses into understanding the mind of God and how He feels about us. In the bible, Ephesians 2:10, tells us we are His workmanship created in Christ Jesus. Can you grasp the meaning of this? Still think you were created by accident or chance: No way! You were planned and hidden in the heart and mind of God from the beginning.

Do you know or believe that God put His glory upon you? Do you know how precious you are to Him? You are marvelous and wondrously made. We were created from His mind, after His own image. The universe, stars and planets all retain their own glory, yet none of these compare with the glory of mankind whom the Lord takes great delight in.

Another evidence of glimpses of God is when you look out of the window at the sky. It changes colors all day long. The wind whips through and around the clouds changing their shapes throughout the day. The sky also changes with the seasons and each sun rising. Every morning God paints a new picture for us to enjoy from His hand, unfolding in part, the mind of God. Do you get a glimpse of Him from what is made or seen yet?

We were created to praise God. Hallelujah is the highest praise that we can give to God. In giving reverence, respect, honor and gratitude to Almighty God for everything He is, we also praise him. We gain new enjoyment as our relationship with Him continues to grow. God in heaven with His angels rejoice over the praises and worship of mankind. God sends His angels from heaven which were also created, to join in with our praise and worship. God also gives His angels charge over us to protect us as believers

WHAT IS SEEN OF GOD THROUGH OUR LORD JESUS CHRIST

All spiritual blessings are yours as believers. God has chosen us through Him before the foundation of the world. Blessed be the God and Father of our Lord Jesus Christ, who has blessed us with all spiritual blessing in heavenly places in Christ. (Ephesians 1:3-5). Read these scriptures from your bible and pray them for yourself. God will bless you with all spiritual blessing that are in Christ Jesus as a believer. These too are awesome glimpses of God through his Son Jesus Christ that we have been given already and established before the foundation of the world. Therefore this is no greater mystery than coming into the knowledge of the word of God. Read Acts 2:29-36. So much about Himself has been revealed as we study the bible and the words of God. His word was given to man to know, perceive, understand and receive glimpses of Him as He is.

God, the Father of the Lord Jesus Christ, covered His glory in the flesh of His son Jesus when He was on earth. Now however, He must reveal Himself in part because of the limitations caused by sin within our mortal bodies. Christ speaks through His believers, apostles, prophets, evangelists, pastors and teachers for the perfection of the saints and for the work of the ministry. All this builds up the body of Christ until we come into the unity of the faith and the knowledge of the Son of God. (Ephesians 4:11-13). This is the five-fold ministry of the mystery of Christ revealed by the Holy Spirit. This is how Christ can dwell in your hearts by faith. Christ has given us glimpses of how He operates through the Holy Spirit. The Lord God promised He will pour out His Spirit upon all flesh. Read Joel 2:28-29, and pray to God that He will pour out the Holy Spirit upon you.

WHAT IS SEEN BY GOD..
OUR FAITH

Our faith is believing, expecting and trusting in the whole word of God as written in the bible. We believe in the birth, death and resurrection of our Lord Jesus Christ. He is alive today. We have faith in the Father, the Son Jesus and the Holy Spirit with all our heart. The Lord sees our faith, and moves throughout whatever we go through in life with supernatural power from God in Christ Jesus, the Anointed One. Your healing, deliverance, salvation and our daily provisions with the love of God have already been given to us through the shed blood of Jesus Christ at the cross when He was crucified. Jesus paved the way for us to freely receive miracles of love and glimpses of God through His grace and mercy. These things are freely given to us when we accept His Son Jesus as Lord and Savior of our life. In the mist of our faith was created the desire to praise and please God.

WHAT IS SEEN BY GOD THROUGH HIS PEOPLE

We were created to praise God. Hallelujah is the highest praise that we can give to God. In giving reverence or respect, honor and gratitude to Almighty God increases the ability to receive more intimate glimpses from Him. This in turn will increase the joy you will receive in your walk with God building your confidence, faith and enriching your relationship with Him. God in heaven with His angels rejoices over the praises and worship of His people, especially when we are on one accord. God sends His angels from heaven to join in with us in the praise and worship of God. God is present and illuminates His people by allowing them to feel His presence in a mighty way when we praise Him. God also gives His angels charge over us to protect us a believers.

Today Satan wages war with us because God loves us. He continuously tries to keep us blinded so we can't get a glimpse of God. Sin is his weapon. This condition is what caused the darkening of our vision and accounts for us receiving only glimpses of God at the present time.

In Genesis 9:11-16, the bible tells us that God established His covenant or promise with mankind. He swore that no more would all flesh be cut off by the waters of a flood to destroy the earth because man became so wicked. The darkness of sin that Satan instigated caused God to bring the flood in the first place. Whenever it rains you see a rainbow right? This was done to remind God of the covenant or promise He made with the earth, mankind and all living creatures. He never wanted to be separated from us but intended for mankind to be the best part of His creation which angered Satan and made it necessary for God to make another plan that would defeat him forever.

GOD'S PLAN FOR MAN

I know the plans I have for you, of peace and not evil,
to given you an expected end. (Jeremiah 29:11)

Where do we go from here? Glimpses of God are yet unfolding. God always has a plan. (Ephesians 3:9-11) It was His plan from the beginning that man should and would be with Him. His desire and intention was for us to work in cooperation with Him ruling the earth on which we live. He made the garden of Eden for Adam to take care of. God watered it so things would grow for us and to feed us. During this time man had direct contact with God not just glimpses. Adam not only saw God's works but also had an intimate relationship with Him which gave Adam unhindered revelations and understanding of God's thinking and heart towards mankind. God gave man dominion over all He made (Genesis 1:28). This included power over our enemy Satan. It was Satan who brought sin into this world by deceiving Adam and Eve, the first man and woman. He used subtlety and deceit on them and caused them to disobey God in order to regain his station in the world. Remember at one time Satan was called Lucifer. He was a very powerful angel of God. During creation he fell by rebelling against God in his pursuit to take over heaven.

His name was changed to Satan and he forfeited his dominion of the earth.

Man's disobedience in breaking the command of God to not eat from a certain tree in the Garden of Eden destroyed the original plan of God. God wanted man to dwell with Him and see Him as He is. This is why we see in part and know in part, getting glimpses of his glory.

God restored our preeminence over the work of his hands through the sacrificial death of Jesus Christ. God gave us a chance to be with Him again by coming Himself in the form of a man. He sent Jesus, His son, who was without sin to defeat our enemy Satan. The death of Christ restored our position with God. How was this accomplished you ask? It was accomplished when Jesus, the only begotten Son of the Father died on the cross and resurrected from the dead. He took the power of Satan away from him and gave it back to believers. When you believe in your heart and confess with your mouth that Jesus is Lord then and only then are the scales of darkness removed from our eyes. Things that have been hidden are revealed with more clarity so that you can begin to receive glimpses of God in greater manifestations.

God has a plan and purpose for your life. He made a plan to redeem mankind back to Himself by sending his own Son, Jesus who is a part of Himself. Jesus who is without sin came to save and redeem us from our sinful condition by taking back the power from Satan and restoring our sight naturally and spiritually. It is Jesus who gave sight to the blind and brought the light of God back into our souls (John 1:4-9). Satan birthed through sin the enmity that broke our fellowship with God, shadowing our relationship with Him and caused us to lose the unhindered presence of Him we once enjoyed.

... Blinded

People without understanding; which have eyes and see not
Jeremiah 5:21

Today Satan wages war with us because God loves us. He continuously tries to keep us blinded so we can't get glimpses of God. Sin is his weapon. This condition is what caused the darkening of our vision and accounts for us receiving only glimpses of God at this present time. Sin brought devastating results in the world. Satan was given power to kill, steal and destroy what God love because of disobedience. Satan has been able to blind us to the goodness and presence of God because our first parents, Adam and Eve, forfeited their rightful place with God. They were in the presence and fellowship of God at all times. They were deceived being drawn in by Satan's subtle craftiness. He lied to them about eating the forbidden fruit.

The bible calls him Satan, the wicked one, the son of perdition, the enemy or adversary of God and man. When you have been blinded you have been tricked or hit unexpectedly. Something or someone has caused you to look another way, losing your focus or direction. Sometimes it can just be an area of ignorance (Acts 17:30). The bible tells us we perish from a lack of knowledge. The prince of this world whom the bible calls Satan took advantage of us through his skillful use of deceit by blinding us and hindering our ability to perceive the nearness of God (2 Corinthians 4:3-4,6). Satan is very cunning and skillfully uses deceit that makes it impossible for us to know that when we agree with him it darkens our sight of God. Sin always leaves a mark behind.

When you lose your sight you have lost the light and will automatically follow what comes naturally. When we choose to call things made by the hands of men god, giving them first place in our lives whether it's our jobs, kids, husbands or wives then they become our god. When we forget our hands are fashioned by God, we have been blinded. Don't be blinded by the idols and things of the world. When we give our attention to everything else and not to the Lord who created us, our destiny is being held up. In Acts 17:22-30 the bible declares when we worship idols we worship what we know not. What foolishness is this? Who has bewitched you? Paul the servant of God declared to the people that they ignorantly worshipped God. God made all things and is Lord of heaven and earth which is not made by man's hands. Perhaps this is why God gives us only glimpses of Himself presently. In this mortal flesh we cannot perceive nor contain any more than what has been revealed.

Sin is the opposite of whole. A hole in the soul of man is what is left. This hole or emptiness can only be filled again by God. I know you have felt this emptiness at times in your life. Perhaps late at night when all is quiet you may wonder what life is all about. Perhaps nothing makes sense to you anymore. He must breathe on you again so that you can become a living soul, alive from the dead and alive unto the things of God. This is your destiny to be one with God. When the Lord breathes upon you again by the Holy Spirit it will restore your spirit (St John 3:3-8). We have been separated and blinded by the darkness of sin and Satan. Remember God sent the light. Jesus is the light. Without God...no light, only darkness prevails as the winner of the soul. The further we move away from God the less light we have. Therefore our sight is hindered limiting our perception to the majesty of God.

The knowledge of good and evil has been revealed and is now placed into the hands of mankind who has stepped out of the light of God's presence being blinded. Sin brought this separation. Darkness began to hinder our sight and desire to be with God. Satan the enemy of God and man, took the opportunity that was forfeited by Adam and Eve by their disobedience to God to bring death, sickness and disease into our world, bodies and lives including shortening our life span. (Genesis 3:22). This still goes on today until the restitution of all things come. Satan is the chief reason of our blindness and limited perceptions and misalignment with God. We have been blinded by Satan who cause the separation between us and God. It is because of him, Satan, we are not abel to bear the glory of God in these bodies in the fullness as we once did. Now w have to wait until the one who brought the darkness is chained. For now we must inhabit these time restricted, limited and mortally infirmity filled bodies.

Sin makes our bones and bodies deteriorate allowing them to be afflicted with sickness and disease. God sent Jesus His Son to overcome sin for us which caused this malady. This overcoming is made manifest in God's goodwill towards men. God our Father sent Jesus to heal and recover what was lost and forfeited by sin. Our imperfections for the present are merely shadows of the glory we will behold one day. (Revelation 21:1-7). We are only able to comprehend the things in the spirit going on at times because Satan has blinded us to the glory of God. He wants to be our god. Whenever we attribute the things made by our hands to be greater than God, we ascribe to Satan as god. We have been not only blinded but also greatly deceived.

Pray this prayer with me if you desire to regain your sight. I will decrease and declare your blessing. Father God, in the name of Jesus, forgive me for allowing stumbling blocks to keep me away from my relationship with you. Lord help me to become more focused and connected with you so I can be more obedient to your voice. Lord send your Holy Spirit upon me to help me make the right decisions in my everyday life. Move the darkness and blindness Satan has brought upon me in my life.

Renewal of Sight

Preach deliverance to the captives and
recovering of sight to the blind.
Luke 4:18

How did we lose our sight? First we need to understand that we had something that could be lost and that it is valuable. Light is very important. We can't move ahead or see where we are going without it. This was the first thing our enemy, Satan, tried to distinguish. He wanted to put the light out knowing the importance of it. Without the light of God who lighted every soul that enters into the world, we would be very easy to control and manipulate. (St. John 1:1-9). Satan then would be able to keep hidden from us the manifestation of God's wonderful glories in us.

Renewal of sight and recovering of sight to the blind can only be accomplished by a believing faith in what Jesus, God's only Son did for us on the cross at Calvary. Jesus death on the cross fulfilled the will of God the Father in every area of our lives. His death and resurrection opened again the way for us to have a relationship with Him and to open our understanding of spiritual things. God so loved the world He gave. (St. John 3:16). Giving is His greatest joy.

Jesus is the light of the world. Christ is the light inside our soul.

Light reveals the things of God to men. Light disperses the darkness. You can't hide when the light is on. Satan our enemy loves darkness. If your find that you love the darkness or things pertaining to it, step out into the light. God will shine the light upon you. Jesus was sent to dispel the darkness of Satan. Jesus came to restore our sight so we can once again enjoy the presence of God, being touched by Him again. This light allows us to behold the beauty of the Lord. Being touched by God is what brings the renewal of our sight and brings the light of God back into our spirit. In the bible, Ephesians 4:23-24, tells us to be renewed in the spirit of your mind. This means being renewed in the thoughts of your mind by the word of God, the bible. Your mind becomes open to receive glimpses of God. You begin to change because the light of God enters in or is turned on. Satan can no longer hold you captive. (2 Corinthians 4:4). The Spirit and nature of God takes up residence in you. No longer will you chase after the desires and pleasures of the flesh with the same intensity they will slowly dissipate. No longer will these things of the world have the power to satisfy your soul. You will begin to hunger after the things that please God instead. In Greek the word for renewed means the whole course of life is new and flows in a different direction. (2 Corinthians 5:17-18), tells us if any man be in Christ he is a new creature, old things pass away. God is now calling forth His people to come out of darkness into His marvelous light. Jesus is the light and wants His glory to fall upon you and be in you. The more people we help bring to Jesus, the light, the brighter we will shine. Allow the Lord to renew your life and accept Him as Lord and Savior. You will never be the same, I promise you.

Ask the Lord to open your eyes to behold wondrous things out of His law, the bible (Psalms 119:18). You will begin to understand the things of God and see them the way He does. Your mind will be illuminated with the light of God, which is the spirit of God. Your glimpses of God will increase, widen and deepen as you seek a closer relationship with Him. He holds our good and all that is good. When

He sent Jesus, His Son, it was declared by His angels, "peace on earth, goodwill towards men", (Luke 2:11-14). Does this sound like someone that is angry with you? No, this is God's mind toward you then and now, He does not change. He is the same yesterday today and forever. (Hebrews 13:8).

He wants you to know Him. He wants a relationship with you. He wants you to tell others about His goodness after you have experienced it for yourself. He invites you to taste and see of His goodness. I promise you when you do, you will never be the same. (Psalms 34:8). This is the renewing of sight. Sight gives understanding and the knowledge of God which increases our ability to perceive the things of God in new and refreshing ways.

THE WORD OF OUR TESTIMONIES

And they overcame him, Satan, by the blood of the Lamb and by the word of their testimony, and they loved not their lives unto death. (Revelation 12:11)

That old serpent, called Satan, and the devil, which deceives by blinding the whole world has been defeated. (2 Corinthians 4:4). God and His Christ have over Satan and all his hosts as predicted in the plan of God with the death, burial and resurrection of Jesus Christ our Savior. To the saints, the accuser of the brethren, Satan has been cast down into the earth. Our faith in the finished work Christ did for us on the cross bombards the forces of darkness and it's dominion over man's spirit. When our eyes are opened to receive glimpses of God, the spiritual realm and reality of this warfare becomes more obvious. This warfare continues today.

These stories are about the demonstrations and testimony of the power of God through Christ by healing and miracles. These stories are true as told by Larry, a man of God gifted with the ability to demonstrate healing's and miracles through the power of the Holy Spirit. The power of God is at work in the lives of people who are in need of healing and miracles in their bodies right now, today.

This testimony is about a woman who is pregnant. Shortly after she delivered her baby, the organs in her body began to shut down. She was taken to intensive care unit immediately. When I came to work the doctor of this patient wanted to talk with me. He asked me to go to intensive care and pray for his patient. The doctor told me there is nothing more they could do for her, she is dying and tears came running down his face. I responded, "I will go and pray for your patient". I approached the unit walking down the hall talking with God and praying in tongues the language of the Spirit of God that He gives to believers, not knowing what will happen. As I arrived on the unit, the Holy Spirit said, "listen very carefully to what I am going to tell you and do everything I say". I asked her nurse if I could see the patient. Before walking into the room the nursing supervisor, who I knew was on that night asked what was going on and why I was here. I explained to him the reason for my visit. He spoke with the patient's nurse who told me the patient is on a ventilator and in a coma with blood clots in her legs. Her blood levels were abnormal and all her organs are shutting down. The nurse took me to the room and left closing the door allowing me to pray for the patient.

The Lord spoke to me and said, "My son I need you to look into the spirit of this woman and see what is going on". The Lord opened my spiritual vision and I saw spirits around the room. The Lord said, "I want those demonic spirits gone right now". I spoke in the name of the spirits, "I bind up every principality and power and rulers of darkness out of this room and off of her in the name of Jesus. The blood of Jesus moved supernaturally throughout of her entire body that no weapon that is formed against her shall prosper" You see, first we must bind the power of Satan up in the name of Jesus. Remember Satan is the one who brings sickness and disease and Jesus defeated his power. In this we take authority over the power of Satan. I kept praying the prayer of faith for the Lord to destroy the demonic attack off of her body for about fifteen minutes. The Lord then spoke, "Now son you can pray the prayer of faith believing in her miracle. "The Lord showed me what was really going on inside of her. The blood was moving radically and the blood clots were in both of her legs. He then spoke, "I want everything in her body to be back to normal". In the name of Jesus move throughout the blood clots and dissolve them in both legs by the blood of the Lamb and the word of our testimonies the Lord spoke again, "I want the patient out of that coma". "I said, "Lord in the name of Jesus take hold of her spirit and bring it back from the other side to earth. Lord Jesus send forth your Holy Spirit inside of her body and start your healing to saturate throughout her organs bring wholeness back into them in the name of Jesus". This continued until every area of her body that Satan had bound was loosed and his power destroyed off of her. The Lord spoke again saying, "Son I thank you for what you have done now she shall live and declare the works of the Lord". God wanted to give her a testimony to His goodness and power that she could share with others and into deeper glimpses of God.

I opened the door to her room and sat down with the nursing supervisor and told him what God had just done for this patient and what He was going to do each day for her. The Lord had me write it down to give to the supervisor and her doctor to show them what God would do for the patient so they would believe in the Almighty and the power of His Christ. Everyday God did something. He had me write, day one: the blood level would become normal, later that evening the blood clots will be gone, One the next day in the morning the patient will be out of the coma. In the evening the organs will start working normal again. The next day in the morning the patient will off of the ventilator and have normal readings. These things happened in this order. This same evening she will be sitting up in the bed ready to be discharged back to a regular unit. The next day give the baby to the mother and discharge them home. The patient wanted to see me and ask questions. The Lord said, "Now my son just tell her she was on the way out of here but the Lord came to her rescue; will you receive Him into your life?". We prayed the sinner's prayer and she received Christ.

This is just one testimony of the glory of God. He never does things the same way, each time it has been different. Nothing can be done without Him. He must lead and guide you every step of the way. When you obey His voice you get dynamic testimonies to glorify Him not yourself. This one testimony gives evidence of the truth of the scriptures that say we overcome by our testimonies, these things are done that we might believe in the love and power of God and His Christ and receive GLIMPSES OF GOD every day.

On another occasion one my sisters in the Lord wanted me to pray for her girlfriend who had to have open heart surgery. While I was listening to her the Holy Spirit started talking to me and said, "I would like for you to join me for spiritual surgery for her instead". I asked the Holy Spirit, "So what do you mean?. The Holy Spirit spoke and said, "Son whatever I say to you just do it. First I want you to pray the prayer of faith for her and plead the blood of Jesus Christ over and inside of her body". Then the Holy Spirit said, "Son you need to see her first so turn your head the other way". The Lord showed me an open vision of a short lady lying down asleep. The Holy Spirit said, "Son are you looking at her? I began to describe to my sister in the Lord what she looks like and she said, "How do you know?" I told her the Holy Spirit showed me an open vision that shined a light for me to see her inside and out. The Holy Spirit said to me, "It is very important that you do everything I tell you because her life is counting on you". I told the Holy Spirit "In that case let's get started". The Holy Spirit instructed me to first extend my hand near her heart and pull her heart out. I was very unsure about what the Holy Spirit was telling me to do. The Holy Spirit said, "Now watch this". A hole was opened up inside of her chest and I could see her heart beating. The Holy Spirit said, "Now take her heart out right now". My hands were going toward her heart. I went to grab her heart and the heart itself was detached from the arteries and veins with chains all over them. I took the heart and asked the Holy SPirit what I was to do with it. The Holy Spirit said, "Put it on the table". I looked at her body where her heart was suppose to be and saw no blood on her chest or anywhere else. I looked at the heart on the table and saw it beating with no blood. The Holy Spirit said, "Now reach up into heaven and pull out a handful of hyssop from heaven". I looked at my hands and there was something running through my hands and down my fingers. The Holy Spirit said, "Now pour the hyssop inside of her chest where her heart was and also pour the hyssop over the heart on the table. Now pray over her body again that she is healed by Jesus stripes already and grab the heart off of the table. Pray that this is a brand new heart in the name of Jesus. It is time to put the heart back inside of her. Put the heart near the opening where the heart goes". The arteries and the veins started to unclamp themselves and reattach unto the heart as I watched in amazement what was happening. The Holy Spirit said, "Now pray that she now has a brand new heart like the one she had as a teenager. Plead the blood of Jesus Christ that never loses it's power to saturate throughout her body and heart. She has a brand new heart so ask her friend to go back to the doctor so they can re-examine her heart." The feedback came two or three weeks later. The doctor said this was a miracle and that she no longer has to have open heart surgery for she has the heart of a teenager.

God is awesome as can be and wants a relationship with you on a one-on-one basis. Allow the Lord to come into your heart today, right now by faith. Don't wait. Another glimpse of God's care and concern for us is seen in this testimony. Joan, our sister in the Lord. Her husband Jerry was very ill and dying. He had lived a rough life of drug abuse and developed diabetes and ulcers on his legs. He became a dialysis candidate because of his declining health. Even in this condition God still cares and is concerned about us; no matter what we have done. The mercy of God is everlasting. Jerry's condition continued to deteriorate. He developed gangrene on his leg.

The doctor wanted to amputate his leg to try and save his life. This decision rested with Joan. Before Jerry's health started to decline, he and Joan talked about what his wishes were if his condition did not improve. At this time he also began to have grand maul seizures and needed to have twenty four hour dialysis. Joan gave the doctor permission to operated and amputate Jerry's leg. When he woke from surgery, Joan was worried that he would be angry at her for doing this. She told him, "I did it to save your life". Joan knew that Jesus was a compassionate God and would have mercy on Jerry. He reached out his hand because he could not speak to let her know he was not angry. Joan told Jerry to look inside his heart and mind to make his peace with the Lord. Joan needed to know where he was going if he died. She asked him if he was ready to see Jesus. He had begun to have seizures uncontrollably and was placed on a ventilator. The doctor told Joan he could leave here having those kind of seizures. The Lord had prepared Joan's heart and it was well with her. She was assured Jerry had made his peace with the Lord so she could let the will of God be done even if it meant letting him go. Joan told the doctor to take him off life support. She called for the elders of the church, his family and children. Joan did not break down at Jerry's funeral. People looked at her strangely and did not understand why she was not crying, She simply said "If you know Jesus you don't have to break down and cry". You see she had a relationship with God and understood that when Jerry made his peace with God he was received into glory that day. God does not always do things the way we think or would like Him to do, but He always does what is for the good of all concerned. This testimony was shared to help you to know glimpses of God come in many different ways and circumstances.

When the time was approaching for my prayer partner and co-laborer of this book Larry's wife to leave this earth for heaven, God the Father sent His heavenly host two angels to stand guard at her bedside in the hospital. I witnessed this event by God giving me an open vision. An open vision is a supernatural event into the things invisible that are given to us by God as we walk with Him. Angels are supernatural beings who do the will of God in heaven. The bible tells us they are sent to minister to those who have been adopted by God the Father, because they believed Jesus is His Son unto salvation. We become sisters and brothers of Jesus when you accepted Him as God's only Son. Right then and there you are adopted into His family and become the children of God. Therefore, when we leave this earth the angels of God are sent to escort us to heaven. These angels were very large, standing as tall as the ceiling in the hospital room and were on each side of her bed. They had a wing span that was as wide as the bed was long. When they opened their wings she was completely covered and protected. This is why the bible says, Be not forgetful to entertain strangers, for thereby ye have entertained angels unknowingly. (Hebrews 13:2). God has opened our eyes to see within the spiritual realm (Ephesians 1:19-20). The God and Father of our Lord Jesus Christ, the Father of glory, may give unto you the spirit of wisdom and revelation in the knowledge of Him. Read Ephesians 1:17-20 from the bible and pray this prayer to ask God to open up your eyes and give you understanding of the riches of His saving, healing and deliverance power.

Healing and Miracles

He was wounded for our transgressions, He was bruised
for our iniquities the chastisement of our peace was
upon Him, and with His stripes we are healed.
Isaiah 53:5

A glimpse of God in healing and miracles requires faith. Believing and trusting in the Father, the Son and the Holy Spirit. This will happen to you as you read, meditate and believe the bible is the word of God. Your appetite for the word of God and prayer will have increased by now. A desire will grow in you to be obedient to the voice of the Lord which is His word, the bible. Do what the Holy Spirit of God is telling you to do, remember He is the third person. He will give you illumination or the ability to perceive the things of God. Prayer using the blood of Jesus and in the name of Jesus with the anointing of Christ who is the great physician, healer and miracle worker will work by your faith in Him. The Lord needs a vessel that He can use. Are you willing to be used of God in an awesome way? If the answer is yes, get ready to be blessed and to be a blessing to others.

Jesus touched many and healed them. Healing restored not only their bodies but also their sight. The darkness of Satan was cast out of them. For this cause Jesus was given to us to destroy the works of darkness, granting us glimpses of God once again.

Healing is a supernatural manifestation of the Spirit of God. Miraculously He enters the body and brings healing and deliverance of disease and infirmities to the whole person. It is the power of God that destroys the work of sin and Satan's darkness brought into the world that destroys the human body.

A miracle is the supernatural event that goes beyond natural forces bringing back wholeness to the body or mind. Healing and miracles are supernatural acts of God divinely interceding on a person's behalf to bring about a miraculous cure. All through the bible, Jesus Christ healed all manner of sickness and diseases. Prayer for healing and miracles for people starts out with a desire to pray for people. Ask God for the gift of healing and the working of miracles. Pick up your bible and turn to the concordance in the back of your bible. Read all the scriptures on healing. Meditate on the scriptures for knowledge in God's word. Start applying the word. The manifestation of the Spirit is given to every man to profit in the things of God. (1 Corinthians 12:7-11). Your relationship with the Lord is the key purpose for intimacy with God. Listen for the voice of the Lord while you are praying or meditating. Have a talk with God. Sometimes it takes a while for God to speak to you so continue to pursue Him. When you begin to hear the voice of God listen very carefully for the Holy Spirit's instructions and do them.

God wants to show you who He really is. Enjoy your relationship with Him and allow His plan for your life to come into full manifestation. Whenever you feel your body getting sick, start now to pray for yourself or someone else. If you see no results call for the church elders to pray the prayer of faith concerning this matter. (James 5:14-16). Romans 8:26-27 says, "It is the Spirit that helps our weaknesses for we know not what we should pray". The Spirit of God makes intercession or prays for us. He searches our hearts and knows what the mind of God is concerning us and prays according to His will. Say this prayer to yourself, Lord create in them a clean heart and renew your Holy Spirit within. Use your faith and focus on your spirit inside of you. Lord Jesus, bind up every principality, power an ruler of darkness in the name of Jesus off your people and that no weapon that is formed against them shall prosper. Here you are taking the authority God has given you as a new creature in Christ over the spirit of the devil who Jesus has defeated (Isaiah 54:17). Continue to pray, Lord we plead the blood of Jesus to move through their blood stream their cells, bones, organs and their mind and heart and whatever part of the body that needs healing. Lord heal your people by the blood of the Lamb and the word of their testimony. Father God in the name of Jesus, release your healing anointing throughout their bodies and heal all manner of sickness and disease. Rebuke the devourer for your name sake and put a hedge of fire of protection upon them. Lord use them in a awesome way so God can get the glory over their life. This will be the start of their testimonies. Lord send your Holy Spirit throughout their whole body so they can experience the power and anointing of God inside their being. If you do these things my brethren you shall never fail and the gift of God will overflow within you enlarging your capacity to receive greater Glimpses of God.

Now may the peace and grace of our Lord Jesus Christ be upon you as you take the next step into greater revelations of God.

I AM A DIAMOND

In the hands of The Lord, He is the Master Craftsman, I was created.

This diamond was created for a special purpose.

God took many years to perfect it, chiseling....honing...buffing and sculpting a little here and there to create His masterpiece.

This diamond was not on display for all to see.

He kept it in His secret place, and only took it out to admire it's rare beauty and brilliance.

Daily the Master Craftsman would take His diamond out for His pleasure and His eyes only.

He admired what He had created and would speak kindly to the diamond reminding it how beautiful it was created.

Occasionally...rarely He would let His real friends take a peek at His prized possession.

One day the Master Craftsman decided to let His friends see His glory and masterpiece,

There was none like it in the whole world...ONLY ONE...His diamond.

Only His real friend would know of the diamonds real value and worth to the Master Craftsman. His real friends knew of the Master Craftsman standard of excellence in all that He put His hands unto.

If the Master Craftsman saw it was good...then it was good. His friends dared not try to bargain or offer a trade to the Master Craftsman for the diamond.

The Master Craftsman, wanted to put His diamond on display in the best of settings, to bring out the brilliance of His diamond.

This diamond He kept hidden from hungry eyes, thieving eyes and the lust of men's heart who only wanted the diamond to sell or give to their worthless fellows.

This diamond God kept hidden in His secret place...not easily discovered by passer-bys or happen chancers.

Only the true seekers could peer at the brilliance of the diamond, hoping that perhaps a glint or rays of it's beauty could somehow transform them or pierce the darkness of their lonely hearts.

This diamond could only be found by true seekers...him who knew the value of the prize possession of the Master Craftsman and would protect and cherish the diamond as He did.

In the diamonds fear and reluctance of being seen or possibly belonging to another....rolled itself to the edge of the table and fell into a pile of ashes hoping to hide itself. But the diamonds brightness shined through the darkness of the ashes.

The Master Craftsman saw it gleaming and picked up the diamond putting it into the palm of His hand.

"Why did you seek to hide yourself diamond", He asked. Then He began to gently blow the ash off of the diamond...one...two...three times. All the ash was gone.

There was no need to wipe or rinse the diamond off...you see... For nothing unclean could stick to the diamond made by God, the Master Craftsman and covered with the Holy Spirit.

"No need to fear little diamond to belong to another " said the Master Craftsman, "for I promise I will never leave or forsake you".

For in the deep facets of your brilliance I have written my name... that NO MAN can change

JESUS......

All scripture references are from the King
James Version of the Holy Bible.

St. John 3:16; 3:7-8; 20:22; 1:4-9; 3:3-8; 1:1-9
Acts 2:2-4; 2:29-36: 17:30; 17:22-30
Revelation 5:8; 8:3-4; 21:1-7; 12:11
Exodus 33:17-23
1 Corinthians 13:9; 12:7-11
Genesis 1:3,26; 9:11-16; 1:28; 3:22
2 Corinthians 4:7; 4:3-4,6; 4:4; 5:17-18
Ephesians 2:10; 1:3-5; 4:11-13; 3:9-11; 4:23-24
Joel 2:28-29
Jeremiah 29:11; 5:21
Luke 4:18; 2:11-14
Psalms 119:18; 34:8
Hebrews 13:8
Isaiah 53:5; 54:17
James 5:14-16
Romans 8:26-27

Printed in the United States
By Bookmasters